# Hunting Dogs

## A PHOTOGRAPHIC TRIBUTE

Russell A. Graves

Published by

**krause
publications**

700 East State Street • Iola, WI 54990-0001
715/445-2214 • FAX: 715/445-4087   www.krause.com

Please call or write for our free catalog of publications. Our toll-free number to place an order or obtain a free catalog is (800) 258-0929.

Library of Congress Catalog Number: 2002105106
ISBN: 0-87349-361-3

# Dedication

To Garry…
I could not ask
for a better friend.

# Contents

# Acknowledgments

I am a man who is indebted to all who assisted me in this project. I fear that once I start listing people I may leave out someone. Therefore, I will start with the easy ones and forgive me if I inadvertently left you out.

First, I would like to thank my wife Kristy and our beautiful daughter Bailee for affording me the time to go on the countless forays to amass all of the stories and photos included in this book.

Thanks to Don Gulbrandsen of Krause Publications for helping this project come to light and to Tracy Schmidt, also of Krause, for her assistance through the completion of this book.

Donna Novak was extremely helpful in suggesting grammatical and stylistic changes in the manuscript in its initial stages.

No amount of praise can come close to repaying all those who allowed me to tag along with them and their dogs on the many hunting trips I made while working on this book. In no particular order, I will try to thank you all. First the upland bird hunters: Scott Sudkamp, Dane Fuller, Silas Ragsdale, Glen Sanders, Gary and Lenora Ryun, Kyle Allen, Jerry Robinson, Craig Reed, Jeff Rash, Garry Mills, Henry and Sara Hearne, Billy Perkins, and Craig Hunt.

Waterfowl hunters include Mark Meissenburg, Mike Burpo, Mike Bardwell, Lynn Burkhead, Jason Wilson, Derek Wilson, Bryan Lackey, Rodney Gibson, and Dr. Bobby Cox.

Hound hunters who helped me out were Jonathon Burpo, Paul Wayne Bridges, Colonel Rex Denny, USMC, and Susan and Craig Gentry.

I also need to thank spaniel hunters Robert Klasing, and Brandon and Amy Rogers.

I would also like to thank the countless landowners who allowed me to follow their hunters across some of the most beautiful land I have ever seen.

Lastly, I would like to thank my daddy and mother, Harold and Ona, for building and nurturing my love of dogs and the outdoors. In addition, thanks go out to my brothers and sisters, Bubba, Larry, Dee, and Glenda for helping me to become the person I am.

No amount of words can express the gratitude I feel in my heart for all who suggested a picture or a scene or simply gave me a word of encouragement. To all who helped, I will forever be in your service.

—Russell A. Graves

# Prologue

When I think in terms of how I could measure the success of this project, I am overwhelmed. Should I count the hundreds of rolls of film I took resulting in literally thousands of images? Should I count the hours of lost sleep? Compile the time I traveled in the dark to be at a destination before the first hint of sunlight? Maybe I should log all of the miles I drove just to see and hunt with a lab or watch someone's pointers work the dirty edge of a field along an unkempt fencerow?

Perhaps there is no way to judge the success of a project like this one. Oh, I guess book sales would be an indication, but that will only tell me how monetarily successful the book was. I wish there was a concrete way for measuring satisfaction. If there were, for me, it would register off the charts. As I think back to all of the miles I have covered and the film I have burned, I am forever changed by meeting these people and their dogs. Hunting dog ownership is a fraternity—and I have become an honored member.

I am impressed by the intense dedication that the owners have to their dogs and vice versa. There is a distinct simplicity and dedication that a person exhibits in taking a dog that is unsure of its inherited abilities and molding it into a finely tuned athlete capable of nosing a nearly invisible bobwhite quail out of the brush.

Since September 11, 2001, much has been written about how the day's events have everlastingly changed Americans into a more caring people who understand and appreciate the value of life's simpler things. September 11 made many on-the-go-Americans stop in their tracks and look around them in a way that people regularly in touch with the natural world already do, every time they participate in the outdoors.

Having spent so much time out in the field, it is thrilling for me to see the passion that mankind still has for both the outdoors and outdoor sports. There is a strong companionship between dog owners and the animals they train and also a sense of compassion for the animals they hunt. I have met dogs with names which I will never forget such as Sax, Nash, Bud, Skeeter, Pete, and Jet. These dogs have carved out places in my mind that remind me of how great humankind and its dominion over animals can be when its authority is treated in a respectful and honorable way.

The people and the dogs I met during this project enriched my life. I have become a more astute student of the natural world and human nature. So far, I like what I see.

In The Texas Panhandle,

Russell A. Graves
January 14, 2002

# Introduction

*"I had some crazy times with those dogs out on the road. Usually I made them sleep in the trunk of the car, but if it was Ol' Roy, who was really more of a pet than a bird dog, I would let him sleep in my room with me…"*

—Sam Walton, founder of Wal-Mart, on his favorite bird dog

A near inexplicable bond exists between the hunting dog and its master that transcends ordinary pet relationships. It is a bond born out of long hours of training that manifests itself in the field, where countless hours are spent in pursuit of winged rockets, rabbits, and other game.

The dogs are with us to help make our time in the field a little easier. They point, tree, flush, retrieve, and swim. It is work well suited to the dogs that are taken afield, and most of them seem to enjoy their jobs. Whether they are instinct-driven to perform their tasks or they do it in part to please their masters is irrelevant. Because these dogs exist, the outdoor heritage and traditions that make up the sport of hunting are strengthened.

Hunting dogs can teach us many things about life. Not so much in an "in your face," obvious sort of way, but in a more subtle, intellectual fashion.

As a boy, I remember following my pet beagle, Whiskers, as he zigzagged with his nose to the ground. He sniffed incessantly for cottontails through the bois d'arc covered draws and cedar thickets indicative of the great Blackland Prairie's northern edge near Dodd City, Texas. When he found one, there was no doubting his sincerity. His vocal chords inflected a high-pitched bawl that, in beaglese, said, "I FOUND ONE!"

During the big commotion, the rabbit would bolt from its cover and Whiskers would follow in direct pursuit. His confidence in his abilities outweighed my shakiness with my single shot .410. More often than not we would come home with an empty game pouch. Yet that beagle, whether he knew it or not, taught me important lessons that a boy should learn: a love for the outdoors, enthusiasm for the task at hand, the value of sometimes falling short of accomplishing a goal, and the importance of trying again.

As I grew into my teens, hunting dogs continued to teach me more about life than, at that time, I dared to admit. I spent countless hours following two rag-tag bird dogs that belonged to my friend Garry. I recall Garry pulling up to my parents' house many times with a dog box in the back of his beat-up Ford, saying the same two words: "You ready?"

As we followed the pair of dogs in and out of old, overgrown fencerows choked with wild rose bushes and blackberries, we talked. While trailing Buck and Hulk we talked about girls, sports, school, plans, and any other things that teenage boys conjure up. As we boys slowly matured into men and consequences put miles between us, the bond of friendship held just as strong as the first day two pointers were turned loose from the back of a Ford pickup.

The hunting dog is many things to its owner, both a member of the family and beloved pet. It is a friend when hunting solo or a focal point for bonding when friends and family enjoy the outdoors. Good dogs are confidants that listen intently and non-judgmentally while you work out the stress and problems the day sometimes brings. They are a source of unconditional love. Even more importantly, they are eager to share that love with anyone who will allow it.

Hunting dogs are also a link to the past traditions of hunting. They make us slow down enough to remember the important things in life. They evoke the reasons why hunting is such a sacred and time-honored tradition worthy of preservation.

Dogs help us create moments in nature that would be difficult to achieve by ourselves. Things like swinging on a covey rise of bobs or experiencing the Technicolor flush of a ring-necked pheasant would be much more difficult if not for our four-legged friends. Above all, hunting dogs are a source of pride.

I've seen grown men engage in lighthearted, verbal sparring as they talk about how their dog is better than someone else's and can find more coveys of quail. The exchange usually goes back and forth until words turn into an impromptu field trial. Usually the winner gets both a steak dinner and, more importantly, bragging rights.

I have witnessed the beaming grin of a dog owner when their puppy first retrieves a stick or goes on point toward the family cat. Although it may have been by sheer accident, their pride cannot be masked as they brag on the pup's first signs of hunting prowess.

No matter what the breed or activity, hunting dogs hold a special place in our hearts. Cherished memories abound as we think about special moments spent afield with the warm companionship of family, friends, and that favorite dog. Sam Walton thought so much of his setter that he named one of the top selling brands of dog food in the United States after his pal, Ol' Roy.

The old term, "man's best friend," seems somewhat of an understatement where hunting dogs are concerned–ask anyone who has one. Most likely, they will drift back and tell you of a hunting story with a favorite dog. With the telling of the story, the legacy continues and that moment is timeless.

# The Pointers

Highway driving in the Texas Panhandle can be a study in the never-ending emptiness of grass and sky. In this part of the state, one can embrace a spiritual feeling by studying the natural symmetry of everything from the furrowed red dirt to the giant cobalt sky.

It was just a few days after Christmas when I left my home under the star-filled darkness of the rolling plains of Texas to meet up with two quail hunting friends. From horizon to horizon, constellations comprised of light decorated the great palette of sky.

Taking a deep breath I jumped into my truck and began the 45-mile drive ahead of me by stopping at an all-night convenience store to grab a cup of cappuccino. A couple of weeks earlier, Craig Reed, a longtime friend from my hometown of Dodd City, Texas, called to give me directions to the camp. When he mentioned they were going to camp near the tiny settlement of Dumont, he did not think I could find it on my own. After some gentle reassurances, he finally spelled out the directions that would take me to their leased hunting land.

When I pulled up to their travel trailer, Craig and his hunting partner Jerry Robinson were already up and stirring about in the chilly West Texas air. Although still not up, the sun was beginning to paint the eastern sky a muted shade of pink. As I stepped out of my pickup to greet the two with handshakes, a heavy frost crunched beneath my feet. As I scanned the field mixed with bluestem and broom weed, I could make out white patches of snow that were remnants of an earlier storm system. For most of autumn, the area had enjoyed Indian Summer-like conditions, but the day after Christmas, a brutal Canadian cold front had dipped far into the Southern plains. The result was a dusting of fine, powdery snow on the mesquite and prickly-pear-covered hills.

Bird hunters tend to like these conditions. A hard freeze is reputed to take the bitter smell out of the abundant broom and ragweed that engulfs the area during what would otherwise be good quail years. The pungent smell of these forbs gives dogs problems and hampers the ability of their olfactory glands to "nose" quail out of the brush.

While Jerry got the dogs ready for the day's hunt, Craig and I reminisced about times on the Blackland prairie and the antics my friends and I had pulled while in high school under his tutelage. Reed, who started working at my school when I was a freshman, was only 21 years old at the time. Only six years my senior, he is now a peer instead of an authority figure, although I still call him "Coach."

When Jerry finally called for us, eight dogs were loaded in a bright red trailer matching his Chevy Z-71. Craig rode in Jerry's truck while I followed them in mine. We had about five miles to drive to a pasture the two had wanted to try out, but had yet to hunt it that year. Driving out from the camp, I stayed close behind.

Following them, I noticed that every time we slowed down or stopped, I would see a flurry of activity at the back of the trailer. It took a little studying, but I finally figured out what was going on. When we stopped for good, I was ready for action. Grabbing my camera, I pulled up fast behind the rig, jumped out, and began to shoot pictures of the scene. Every time the bird dogs thought we were going to stop, they would put their wet noses through the inch-wide vent holes in the dog box doors and sniff excitedly. Born and bred to hunt, the pointer bird dogs were a picture of anticipation. Fired up for the impending hunt, they all got a head start on the birds by using the most effective tool they have—their noses.

A study in genetic selection, the pointers were there to do what they and their ancestors had been expected to do for centuries. Originating in England around 1650, the breed was developed with a singular purpose in mind—finding and pointing game. Originally hunted in conjunction with greyhounds, pointers were used to find hares. Then when the hounds were unleashed, the hares kicked from cover, and the greyhounds would run them.

It wasn't until the early 1700s that wing shooting became popular in England, and the breed's destiny was solidified. Early bird hunters found the pointer to be as reliable as the English setter and they made easy work of finding and flushing birds.

The exact ancestry of English pointers is open to speculation, but experts suggest that the original breed was derived from various crosses between greyhounds, bloodhounds, and foxhounds. Since then, the lineage has been diluted with the bloodlines of setters to give the breed a milder disposition. Yet the dogs must still exhibit the characteristics of short hair, sturdy build, and splotched color variations of liver or black and white.

Today, the English pointer is the most popular of all the pointing dogs. Energetic, spirited, and friendly, the breed is field hearty and has a stamina that keeps it hunting in all sorts of terrain. From a very early age, the puppies show a penchant for pointing all sorts of crazy things.

A friend once related a story to me about a three-month-old male English pointer he had. The pup was special to the family and was treated differently from the other dogs in the kennel—this one got to come inside the house. The very first time the dog pointed, according to the story, he honed in on the house cat and refused to move from the classic pointing position of nose down, tail-up. From that moment on, the dog was a natural and easy to train. Needless to say, it retained its place in the kennel hierarchy.

The land we were hunting that day had been set aside as Conservation Reserve Program (CRP) land. The CRP program, implemented by the United States Department of Agriculture during the mid-1980s, paid farmers to take highly erodible land out of crop production. The farmers would then plant it in grasses and forbs beneficial to wildlife. As a result, upland birds such as pheasant and quail flourished.

Meanwhile, Jerry turned the excited dogs loose from the trailer's confines. Running around in a frenzy, some of the dogs marked their scent on trees and truck tires, while others sparred in play fights. This particular group of dogs was a study in age diversity. Some were well seasoned, as signified by the gray hair creeping into their coats. Others were experiencing their first season afield and began testing out their noses.

One dog in the bunch was an old female. I could tell she had some age behind her, because she wasn't quite as spry as the others and commanded an air of respect as she socialized with the younger dogs. "That dog's name is Prissy," said Jerry. "I've had her for 14 years now and she is the best dog I have ever owned." For Jerry, a man who knows dogs, his statement was a big one.

Once we started hunting, the dogs were quick to point. "Birds in here!" Reed said, giving verbal commands to the dogs. Watching good pointers work is like watching a well-choreographed football play. One dog finds the birds and the other dogs fall in line and "honor" the one on point. Honoring is a term used to describe a dog's ability, good or bad, to spot one dog pointing and to stop what he is doing until the birds are flushed. A dog that can honor gets to hunt many seasons—the ones that cannot usually find new homes.

Reed slipped up behind a big black and white dog, known as Coot, and nudged him up toward the direction he was pointing. In an explosion of activity, half a dozen brown and black bobwhite quail flushed from the grass. All at once, dogs that just milliseconds before were virtually frozen in their tracks, sprang to life as the sound of beating wings mingled with reports of shotgun blasts.

In a couple of seconds it was over. The hunters were looking around and mentally taking note of where birds fell. In the meantime, the dogs had their noses buried in the grass and were running simultaneously in order to pick up a scent. Although not the one to initially point, Prissy was the first to find a bird and trot it over to Jerry. Wagging her tail with excitement, she graciously submitted the bird to Jerry as he knelt beside her.

"Can you take a picture of us?" he asked.

"Sure…" I said as I fiddled with the settings on my camera. While I was composing the photograph, he petted Prissy in a compassionate way that made it clear there was a strong bond and a lot of history between the two. As he took the bird from her mouth, I snapped a couple of shots and promised him prints.

"I don't know how much longer the old girl will be with me," he said in a melancholy tone as he removed his cap and wiped his sleeve across his brow. "I thought about not hunting her this year but I couldn't bear to leave her at home." Prissy seemed slowed down by age, but the years didn't dampen her enthusiasm.

The day ended as quickly as it began. A limit of quail, and the sight of good dogs at work, made it a fruitful trip. Everything was as it could be expected on a West Texas quail hunt—plenty of birds, pretty country, and lots of walking. Before I headed toward my truck, I once again shook hands and thanked the pair for the opportunity to photograph them. I also stopped to pet a dog, which returned my kind gesture with a swab on my hand from its wet tongue.

Time passed and the photos were eventually submitted to magazines. When the first one appeared in a hunting magazine, it was the one I had taken of Jerry and Prissy. Placed prominently in the center of the page, it was something I knew would make the dog's owner proud. Picking up the phone, I called Jerry and told him the news. He seemed happy, but there was also a hint of sadness in his voice. He told me that just a couple of weeks prior, Prissy had died. Sick, old, and beyond healing, she had to be put to sleep. Knowing what it is like to lose a beloved pet, I sympathized with him. At the same time, I knew he would love the final tribute to the dog with which he had spent so much time afield.

*Craig and Coot*

Dogs, especially ones that help connect you with the natural world, hold a special place in a hunter's heart. They are bragged on, and they help connect the times and places that make hunts memorable. Milan Kundera wrote, "…dogs are our link to paradise. They don't know evil or jealousy or discontent. To sit with a dog on a hillside on a glorious afternoon is to be back in Eden, where doing nothing was not boring—it was peace."

One time, I had a group of high school kids on a field trip at the state-owned Matador Wildlife Management Area north of Paducah, Texas. It is some of the best bobwhite quail habitat in the country. It was a drizzly late-October day when a dozen or so teenagers and I were walking amongst the prickly pear and mesquite brush just off a dirt road. While trying to extol the virtues of broom weed or some other type of plant, some movements in the brush caught my eye. Stopping what we were doing, we watched as one of the most beautiful dogs we had ever seen came trotting through the grass.

Wet from the heavy dew, the dog was a picture of athleticism. It had a wide front, deep barrel chest, and a distinct taper from front to back—the dog rippled with muscles. A bright-orange collar accented his rusty color and a docked bobtail of about six inches revealed the dog's breed.

There was a pair of men following the dog, apparently a father and son team, who stopped to talk. The younger one, in his twenties, carried a shotgun, while the gentleman, perhaps in his forties, followed unarmed.

"What kind of dog is that?" asked a student.

The older gentleman, well groomed and dressed in traditional upland game garb turned to the person who asked the question. He quickly told her that it was a German shorthaired pointer, and that he had been a quail hunter for many years. Being from the southeastern United States, an area rich in the tradition of quail hunting, the gentleman explained to us that he didn't carry a shotgun anymore because he received enough enjoyment from watching the dog work—a sentiment shared by many.

Like the English pointer, the German has a storied history that dates back several hundred years. A mix between Spanish pointers, English foxhounds, and German tracking hounds, the shorthair is renowned for its keen nose and intelligence in the field.

During the 1920s, the dog was first imported to the United States. Its first role was that of a multipurpose breed successful at tracking. The dog could be used on raccoons and was a natural retriever on land, as well as water, due to its water repellant coat and webbed feet. A staunch watchdog, it was well equipped with a nose for sniffing out game birds such as grouse and quail.

The color of a German shorthaired pointer is somewhat different from an English pointer. Although variations occur, a typical shorthair is liver and white, often ticked with spots, and its color can range from solid to roan. When mature, the dog is a sturdy breed that stands about two feet high at the shoulders and weighs an average of 55-60 pounds. Although not as common as English pointers, German shorthairs are the favorite of many hunters who want an obedient dog with no aversions to water or other obstacles. Being highly intelligent, German shorthairs are quick learners.

A common way to start training dogs to point at quail scent is to start with a wing. Once, an acquaintance of mine, Jeff, worked a puppy using this method. He used a rod and reel equipped with monofilament line for a rig. He tied a quail wing on the end of the line. The pup, at the time about two months old, knew he was supposed to do something, but could not figure out exactly what. He would see the wing, point for about a second, and run hard to try to get the wing in his mouth. Each time he would get up to the mass of feathers, the rod would be twitched and the wing jerked away. The scene played out like a segment from the cartoon Peanuts where Charlie Brown would run to kick the football and Lucy would jerk it out from under him. Charlie Brown would always miss and land on his back. Each time the dog would get to the wing, he would skid on the gravel and, in a not-so-graceful manner, fall over on his side.

The pup continued his antics for about an hour, and Jeff was obviously getting impatient. Each time he would jerk the wing away, the dog would fall over, then get up and start jumping at the dangling wing. Nipping at it constantly, he would occasionally get his razor sharp puppy teeth into the wing until, eventually, it was just a jumbled heap of feathers.

The sun was sinking fast when it seemed that knowledge finally seeped into the puppy's brain. He pointed and held. It wasn't the prettiest point, but the look on Jeff's face was priceless, and he verbally praised the dog. The hour's worth of frustration and work were now a distant memory, because his pup had finally put knowledge, instinct, and a little bit of experience together. The pup's little tail wagged back and forth in a blur. The two had connected on a higher level and a bond was forming.

"Whoever said you couldn't buy happiness never owned a puppy," once wrote author Gene Hill. Truer words were never spoken.

# The Retrievers

Just ask anyone who has hunted ducks if it isn't as much in-the-field fun as can be had. On the surface, however, the prognosis for such doesn't always seem too appealing. Hunters are up at about 4:30 a.m. and in their blind by 5:30 a.m., after trudging along in chest-high waders. Frequently, they are lugging a heavy shotgun and an even heavier bag of decoys. And did I mention that "perfect" waterfowling weather includes wind-driven rain with near-freezing temperatures?

Once at the blind, you have to rush around to get everything into position, taking into account the variables like wind direction. Ducks, like other birds or airplanes, like to land into the wind. The wind aids in maintaining a measure of aerodynamic lift, while their forward motion slows to nearly a stall.

After all of the factors are figured out, the decoys must be placed. One at a time, they are gathered from a mesh bag, and the weights that keep them in place are unraveled from around the plastic bodies of the ducks. Green-headed mallard drakes are pulled out first, followed by some drab-colored hens along with a few wigeons, and a pintail or two to finish off the mix. Savvy hunters sometimes put out confidence decoys like great blue herons. Confidence decoys are always extremely skittish birds like herons that are meant to cause ducks to think, "Hey, if he feels safe landing there, so can I!"

Ducks, when coming in fast for a landing, cup their wings low in order to reduce their lift and drop altitude fast. Getting closer to the water, they then rock their bodies back and forth to try to slow their descent somewhat before hitting the water. It sounds complicated, but ducks performing this feat are sheer poetry.

Once the decoys are in place, it's time to don your camouflage head net and put on gloves to protect your fingers from the bitter cold often accompanying duck marsh trips. Then, the sun begins to come up and you wait…and wait until legal shooting time.

Suddenly, ducks in the distance are silhouetted against the lightening sky. The call goes out from a carved wooden cylinder with a plastic reed: QUAAACK, QUACK, QUACK, QUACK, QUACK. Breaths heave from deep within lungs to blow through the call, making it sound believable to the area waterfowl. Others in the party watch intently as beaded eyes stare out from a camo cloak at the circling birds. Hot breaths of anticipation mix with the cold air. The ducks make a couple of passes at the decoy spread, checking out its authenticity. On the last pass, they commit to land.

When the caller gives the word, shooters take aim with steel shot and test their luck against winged missiles. Sometimes the hunters hit a bird, but mostly they miss—that's why it's called hunting.

Once a downed duck hits the water, the real work should begin, but thanks to a breed of super dogs, it doesn't. It was for such situations that Labrador retrievers were bred. The breed's foundation was based upon the instinct to go and fetch something.

The breed's origins can be traced back some 500 years to the present-day Newfoundland Island coast on Canada's Atlantic ocean. Early fishermen used a breed called the St. John's dog to help them in the daily chores of hauling in fishing nets and catching fish that jumped astray. The original breed probably got its name from the capitol city of St. John, located on the Avalon Peninsula.

The dogs were well suited to the work presented to them with their thick water-repellant coats, stout bodies, and efficient webbed feet for swimming in the North Atlantic seacoast's strong surf. Cod anglers used the dogs for up to 20-hour workdays to help retrieve fish. In the early days, the St. John's dog existed in two strains—a large dog for working with fishing lines and nets, and a smaller dog that was carried in boats and went primarily for fish.

In early 19th century England, the St. John's dog's importation first began. It was in England that the dog underwent genetic refinements and first got the name Labrador retriever. Although the breed was developed in Newfoundland, geographical confusion evidently led to naming the dog after the island's provincial northern neighbor across the Strait of Belle Isle, Labrador.

In England, the dog was bred for gun work. From the early 1800s to 1885, the primary breeders of the St. John's dog were the second and third Earls of Malmesbury. These two English noblemen continued to import and refine the breed. It was perhaps the third Earl who gave the breed the name that survives today:

"We always called mine Labrador dogs and I have kept the breed as pure as I could from the first I had from Poole, at that time carrying on a brisk trade with Newfoundland. The real breed may be known by having a close coat which turns the water off like oil, and above all, a tail like an otter."

About the same time, elsewhere in England, the Duke of Buccleigh and the 10th Earl of Home were also importing, breeding, and refining the St. John's line of dogs' genetics. Together, they developed the Buccleigh line of Labradors.

In 1882, the third Earl of Malmesbury, in a chance meeting with the sixth Duke of Buccleigh and the 12th Earl of Home, gave them some dogs from his Malmesbury Labrador line. The mixing of bloodlines between the Malmesbury and Buccleigh dogs ushered in the Labrador retriever phenotype that has descended into present day.

During the early part of the 20th century, the breed slowly became popular in England. In fact, they showed up at field events, and competed with other breeds in the retriever group such as curly-coated and flat-coated retrievers. At first, all retrievers in England were shown in the same class. In 1903, the breed was finally granted its own registry in the English Kennel Club.

During World War I, Labradors first arrived in the United States. At first, all of the retriever breeds, including the Chesapeake Bay, the golden, and the Labrador, were lumped into one classification by the American Kennel Club (AKC). It wasn't until the late 1920s, that the AKC finally recognized the Labrador as its own breed. It then established a category in its registry for keeping records on individual animals.

Between World War I and World War II, interest in the breed remained stagnant by American dog owners, largely due to troubles abroad, and domestic challenges such as a prolonged drought and the Great Depression. Post-war prosperity brought about an increased interest in the breed. During the fifties and through the second half of the 20th century, the Labrador's popularity experienced rapid growth.

According to registration numbers compiled by the AKC in 1998, the Labrador was the most popular dog in the United States accounting for 157,936 total animal registrations. The breed is so popular it eclipses the second most popular dog, the golden retriever, by 92,255 animals. However, both breeds are part of the retriever family, along with the lesser-known cousins such as the curly-coat, the flat-coat, and the obscure Nova Scotia duck-tolling retriever.

The Labrador, or Lab as it is regularly known, is a natural companion animal and remains a popular pet. It is a medium-sized dog with a short-coupled and stout body, but is extremely athletic.

As such, it is a very energetic breed suited to family trips to the park, as well as all-day hunts in a duck marsh, or searches for upland game birds. It possesses a broad head and caring eyes that hint at the breed's characteristic level of intelligence. Being extremely loyal, it is no wonder that the Labrador retriever is the favorite among hunters, general dog lovers–even presidents. Presidents Gerald Ford and Bill Clinton both had retrievers that served the country as "First Dogs." Ford had a golden retriever while President Clinton had a Lab.

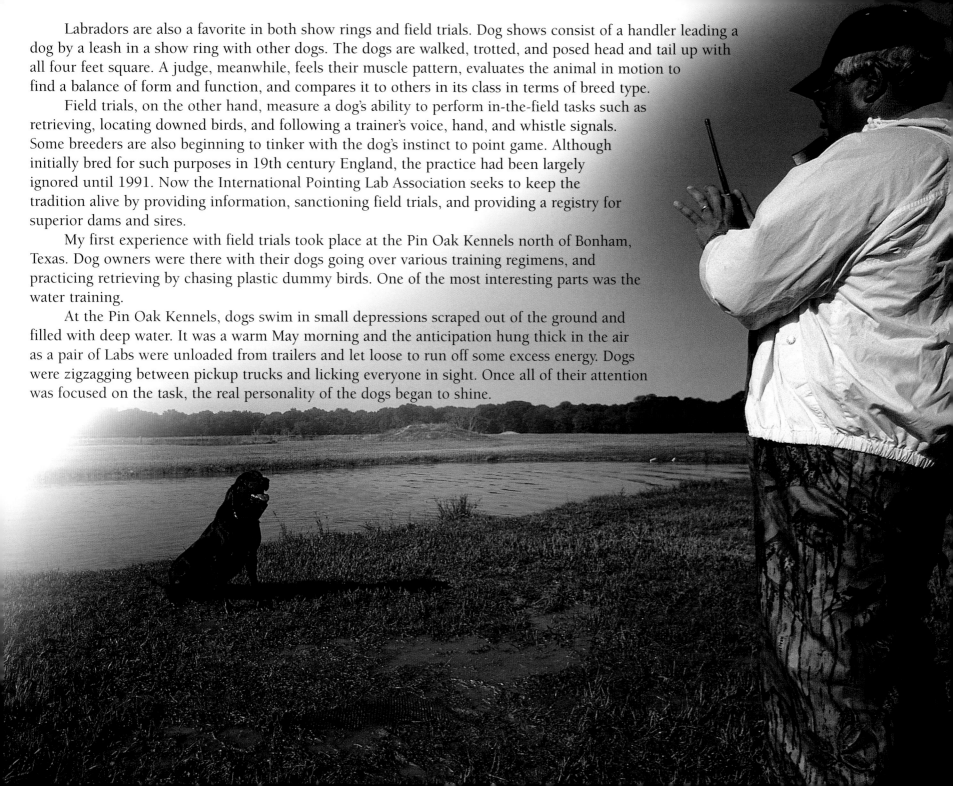

Labradors are also a favorite in both show rings and field trials. Dog shows consist of a handler leading a dog by a leash in a show ring with other dogs. The dogs are walked, trotted, and posed head and tail up with all four feet square. A judge, meanwhile, feels their muscle pattern, evaluates the animal in motion to find a balance of form and function, and compares it to others in its class in terms of breed type.

Field trials, on the other hand, measure a dog's ability to perform in-the-field tasks such as retrieving, locating downed birds, and following a trainer's voice, hand, and whistle signals. Some breeders are also beginning to tinker with the dog's instinct to point game. Although initially bred for such purposes in 19th century England, the practice had been largely ignored until 1991. Now the International Pointing Lab Association seeks to keep the tradition alive by providing information, sanctioning field trials, and providing a registry for superior dams and sires.

My first experience with field trials took place at the Pin Oak Kennels north of Bonham, Texas. Dog owners were there with their dogs going over various training regimens, and practicing retrieving by chasing plastic dummy birds. One of the most interesting parts was the water training.

At the Pin Oak Kennels, dogs swim in small depressions scraped out of the ground and filled with deep water. It was a warm May morning and the anticipation hung thick in the air as a pair of Labs were unloaded from trailers and let loose to run off some excess energy. Dogs were zigzagging between pickup trucks and licking everyone in sight. Once all of their attention was focused on the task, the real personality of the dogs began to shine.

The root of all Lab behavior is a wanton desire to please their master. It seems their whole sense of being is wrapped up in their willingness. During the drill, one dog sat on his haunches and with gentle eyes watched his master, waiting anxiously for a command.

The drill seemed simple: Jump in the water, swim to the white, knobbied training dummy that is about the size of a rolled, big city newspaper, and bring it back to the handler on shore. Once the dummy was pitched into the water, the dog sat fidgeting noticeably. As it stared at the floating hunk of plastic, the handler approached from behind. With a flat hand held stiff as if to deliver a karate blow, the handler held his hand vertically above the dog's head and pointed it in the direction in which to run. When he gave the command, the dog sprang from its seat and bolted towards the pond.

Hitting the water, the dog looked as if he were hydroplaning across its glassy-smooth surface. Never sinking below its jaw line, the dog swam steadily toward the dummy. When the handler blew his whistle, the water-soaked Lab stopped. To face the whistle, he turned around 180 degrees, and started treading water in place. With each successive whistle, the handler pointed to the direction he wanted the dog to swim and the Lab would obey. First left, then right, then back, and forward. The exercise is completely choreographed, yet totally spontaneous. Finally, the dog retrieved the dummy and brought it back to shore, dropping it at the trainer's feet. For his efforts, the loyal Lab got a reassuring head pat and a well-earned, "Good boy!"

Almost two years later, I was on a duck hunt with Mike Bardwell and Lynn Burkhead. Mike, an outfitter and an associate with the Pin Oak Kennels, and Lynn, then the outdoor editor of the Sherman, Texas, newspaper, were both well versed in duck hunting. I walked down and met them at 5:30 a.m. on an old dirt road near my parents' home. Mike suggested that I ride with them the rest of the way to where we would hunt. After opening a gate, we rode in his old four-wheel drive Chevy Suburban down a bumpy trail that intersected a cattle pasture. We made our way to a wide creek bottom and parked amid the brush about 200 yards from some recently flooded grasslands.

After donning waders and a coat, Mike opened the back of his hunting rig and unlatched the portable kennel's door. The dog was hard to see because his coat color matched the blackness of the early morning, but I could hear him running around in the dried grass. We gathered up the gear and walked the last few steps to where we thought the ducks would land.

As we stood in shin-deep water, the sun began to brighten the sky. A day or two earlier, a cold front had pushed ducks down from the northern plains, removing all the clouds as it traveled. The water spread out in a broad oval and cloaked about four acres of grass and young trees. At the northeast end, mud and downed tree limbs were packed together in a classic example of a beaver dam. Beavers, who are fond of shallow lakes, are perhaps the greatest natural contributors of suitable duck habitat in North America.

Shallow water is exactly what puddle ducks such as mallards, wigeons, and wood ducks look for during their annual migration. Puddle ducks prefer shallow waters so that they can tip down to bottom feed on grasses and seeds. Often, while their feet paddle furiously trying to keep their buoyant bodies from popping up out of the water, you can see their rear ends sticking straight up. The other group of ducks, divers (including ring-necked ducks and redheads), prefer large bodies of water to land on and feed. When divers feed, they go under water completely, and sometimes do not resurface for several minutes.

As Mike, Lynn, and I sat, I asked Mike about the dog sitting contently in the cold water just a few feet away. The black lab happened to be a kennelmate of the one I had noticed during the training session at the Pin Oak. Well-trained and disciplined, the dog now before me, Nash, waited in place for Mike's command.

Duck hunting becomes easy with dogs like Nash. Two years old at the close of the 20th century, Nash was already a seasoned gun dog with many hours in the field behind him. While the three of us talked in loud whispers, Nash watched the skies. When he spotted some ducks in flight, he began to fidget and lick his lips—a classic example of Pavlov's experiment. His bright yellow eyes efficiently tracked the fast-flying game as they approached the decoy spread from across the horizon.

Mike and Lynn called in near synchronous bursts while the ducks circled overhead. As the birds cupped their wings and prepared for their final approach, loud reports from camouflaged shotguns pierced the cold, late-November morning. Steel shot flew in multiple bursts from the shotguns, yet only one mallard dropped from the sky—a hen. Nash watched as the bird plopped into the water about 60 yards away. Anxious, he rose to all four feet and stamped his feet excitedly. When Mike yelled, "NASH!" he bounded fast, splashing cold water all around him. He quickly scooped up the harvested bird and brought it back to Mike.

As the morning drew on, the ducks stopped flying and we all decided to call it quits. Mike and Lynn had gotten a few ducks and I had taken some dandy hunt photos. We had trudged about 100 yards to dry ground when I noticed that Nash was holding up one of his back legs. Since it was dark when we had gone into the marsh, I had not noticed it. However, now that it was daylight, I questioned the anomaly.

The previous summer, the dog had hurt his back leg in a training exercise. He was diagnosed as having a torn anterior cruciate ligament. This same injury strikes many human athletes. Several surgeries attempted to repair the injury and succeeded in solving much of the problem. At the time of the hunt, the muscles in his rear hip were still slightly atrophied. He often held it up and simply walked on three legs. It was apparent that the dog wasn't in pain and, like the finest of human athletes, wasn't going to let an injury put him out of the game forever.

If there is such thing as a dog showing heart, Nash could be the poster dog of all gun breeds. I am referring to the desire to beat the odds and overcome obstacles that would stop many in their tracks. Nash had more heart than perhaps any dog I have ever seen. A potentially crippling injury wasn't enough to stop him from doing what he obviously loved.

# The Hounds

When people think of hunting dogs, I suspect most of them think of hounds. Yet, their long ears, drawn out bawl that seems to be a cross between a bark and a howl, and docile disposition make them a favorite not only for hunters, but also for pet owners.

Hounds encompass a wide variety of breeds not just associated with hunting. Bassets, Afghans, greyhounds, whippets, and dachshunds were all developed originally for hunting game of some sort. However, these days, their purpose has somewhat changed from the original prototype.

Greyhounds now chase fake rabbits around pari-mutuel gambling tracks while screaming fans wager money on the short-track race's outcome. Bassets are good pets for many. In fact, one even serves as the Maytag appliance technician's sidekick in commercials. Dachshunds were originally developed to hunt badgers in Germany. In fact, their name directly translates to "badger hound" (dachs: badger; hund: hound). Because of their diminutive stature and long, slender body, their handlers put them in the badger's hole to drag the furbearer out. Although it is doubtful that "weenie dogs" still hunt badgers today, their fierceness for their size and their powerful bark hint at the breed's ancestry. These traits also make them good watchdogs.

My experience with hounds began back before I was a decade old and continued through my early teens. My first cousins, who were close to my age, and their parents would come to visit several times a year. Often, around the Christmas holidays, the whole crew would show up with one of their friends from Dallas who owned some black-and-tan coonhounds. The dogs' owner, an older gentleman whose name escapes me, had a weathered face and a kind, jovial way with kids.

Coon hunters are a different bunch for several, but not altogether, unusual reasons. Most folks who hunt with dogs, whether it is upland birders or waterfowlers, get up at early in the morning and are in the field before the sun crests. Coon hunters, on the other hand, follow a completely different set of rules.

We would get ready to leave the house around 9 p.m. The dogs would get loaded up first in the truck's rear. Then we would make a quick check of our personal gear:

Mud boots: They were supposed to be snug, but not tight. I was always taught that it was best to get boots that were about a size too big. That way I could wear thick wool socks to insulate them during the cold winter nights. In addition, the boots had to be waterproof. I would check mine in a five-gallon bucket of water because an ankle-deep marsh was no place to find out I had a leak.

Clothing: It would need to be warm. Many coon hunters opt for coveralls. The utility of the garment is unsurpassed. Pants and coat made together and they are insulated. In addition, they sport double pockets on the front and they are also equipped with chest pockets and large back pockets.

Light: One of the important aspects of coon hunting is light. The ones we used were like coal miner's lights. The adults I hunted with called them "wheat lights." They were round lights about three inches in diameter with an adjustable beam which threw a spotlight for finding a treed coon or could be set to flood a broad area. The lamp could be clamped onto a helmet or the front pocket of some coveralls and was connected to a rechargeable battery attached to a belt. Fully charged, the powerful lights seemed like they could last forever.

Miscellaneous gear: Aside from the obvious gear mentioned, other gear for the hunt could include a pocketknife for field utility purposes, a small caliber rifle for harvesting the raccoon, a thermos of coffee or hot chocolate, and some snacks.

Did I mention the mules? To hunt raccoons, we rode mules. Jumping mules, in my estimation, are among the most interesting collaborations between God and man. The recipe is simple: one part horse and one part donkey, which combined together form a mule.

Jumping mules serve two unique purposes to the coon hunter. First, they provide a way to follow the dogs without having to put miles on your feet. Second, they can jump a fence, which eliminates the need to ride to gates. Many landowners break their land up into parcels in which they rotate grazing cattle. Barbed wire fences, which are the rule for cattle operations these days, are hard for animals to cross. So someone, somewhere, came up with the idea of training a mule to jump a fence on command, though they won't jump just anytime.

The ones I have had the privilege to ride required the rider to lay a burlap sack over a fence and then give the reins a tug. Rising up on their hind legs, they would lunge forward, clearing the top wire of four-foot-high fences. The burlap sack is significant, because that is what helps cue the mule to jump. If trainers did not use a sack, the mules would jump fences whether or not you wanted them to.

We would ride, and ride, and ride. When you are coon hunting, you don't follow right behind the dogs. Instead, they run out in front, sniff the ground, and bay loudly as they search for their quarry. A throwback to colonial days, coon dogs are highly specialized. Refined over the years, the breed has become a potent combination of agility and stamina tied together by a super-sensitive nose.

The only breed of coonhounds recognized by the American Kennel Club is the black-and-tan coonhound. However, there are five more breeds of hounds that are popularly recognized by the coon hunting fraternity. They are the redbone, bluetick, Plott, English, and the treeing Walker. Of these, the bluetick and the treeing Walker are perhaps the favorites.

We would hunt with blueticks, so named because their coat is a light bluish tint complemented by little specks of black or brown. We followed them for hours. The man who owned the dogs would make us stop on our mules and occasionally sit silently while he listened. Distant bawling would always cause him to turn his head toward the sound. Although I could not tell the difference, he was able to discern the subtleties in the dogs' voices, which separated a casual bark from a signal for a found coon.

"Hunt for 'em," he'd yell. The sound of his voice would cause the dogs to bark with an increased frenzy.

"Arrrrooooooo!" they would always respond, telling him that they had found a raccoon.

Riding in their direction, we would find the dogs jumping excitedly at a big oak's base or some other hardwood tree. If there were low limbs, some of the dogs would even climb up into the tree. Shining our wheat lights onto the bare limbs above revealed the glowing blue raccoon eyes. Sometimes we would harvest the animal with a clean shot from a .22 caliber rifle. In the early to mid-1980s, top-grade coon hides might bring $25-$30 apiece. Most of the time though, we would just look at the animal for a minute and then move on.

Many contemporary coon hunters admit that they are in it for the chase. The motivation for owning hunting dogs is the enjoyment of watching dogs work and spending time training them. There is a great deal of satisfaction in taking a puppy and helping mold it into a fine hunter.

There is little doubt that it was a partial motivation for developing treeing hounds. The other motivation was to catch game. When settlers first fanned out across the eastern United States' deciduous forests, they found that their foxhounds would find game but not tree it. So they set forth to develop a breed with specific traits: the stamina to run long distances, the agility to climb trees, and a strong nose coupled with a stronger hunting instinct. Another important trait is the innate need to hunt in packs, which ensures that the dogs don't separate while hunting.

Every now and then, we would lose a dog, but it would wander back a few days later. In fact, I remember returning many coonhounds to their owners during my adolescence. The hounds would wander up to my parents' country home looking for some attention. Thinking them a little thin, I would give them some fresh food and water and then look at the collar so I could record the owner's name and phone number. A brief call is usually all it took to get a dog picked up and on its way back home. Once home, I am sure they were nursed back to health, given a few days' rest, and once again, given the chance to do what coonhounds love to do—hunt.

The only breed of coonhounds recognized by the American Kennel Club is the black-and-tan coonhound. However, there are five more breeds of hounds that are popularly recognized by the coon hunting fraternity. They are the redbone, bluetick, Plott, English, and the treeing Walker. Of these, the bluetick and the treeing Walker are perhaps the favorites.

We would hunt with blueticks, so named because their coat is a light bluish tint complemented by little specks of black or brown. We followed them for hours. The man who owned the dogs would make us stop on our mules and occasionally sit silently while he listened. Distant bawling would always cause him to turn his head toward the sound. Although I could not tell the difference, he was able to discern the subtleties in the dogs' voices, which separated a casual bark from a signal for a found coon.

"Hunt for 'em," he'd yell. The sound of his voice would cause the dogs to bark with an increased frenzy.

"Arrrrooooooo!" they would always respond, telling him that they had found a raccoon.

Riding in their direction, we would find the dogs jumping excitedly at a big oak's base or some other hardwood tree. If there were low limbs, some of the dogs would even climb up into the tree. Shining our wheat lights onto the bare limbs above revealed the glowing blue raccoon eyes. Sometimes we would harvest the animal with a clean shot from a .22 caliber rifle. In the early to mid-1980s, top-grade coon hides might bring $25-$30 apiece. Most of the time though, we would just look at the animal for a minute and then move on.

After a 15-year hiatus from following coonhounds, I was reintroduced to the sport during the spring of 2000 by a pair of unlikely ambassadors: a 16-year-old country kid named Jonathon Burpo and his grandfather, Paul Wayne Bridges. My introduction to Paul Wayne and Jonathon wasn't a new one. I have known Paul Wayne for a number of years. His younger brother and I grew up and graduated from high school together and, as a result, I have known Jonathon since he was born.

Through the years, Jonathon has grown into a fine young man with an incredible knack for training hounds. The first set of dogs I remember him having was beagles. French for "small," the beagle is a hunting hound whose origins date back to Renaissance-era France and Wales. Developed for hunting hares in Europe, it easily adapted to chasing rabbits once it was brought to the United States.

Jonathon used beagles during his junior high years to chase cottontails through the briar thickets and creek draws near his home. He had a dandy pair of beagles, which, when released together, could nose out rabbits nestled deep in the brush. Beagles, like other hounds, are trained to hunt in packs, because several noses sniffing for scent are bound to be better than one.

When I met with Jonathon and Paul Wayne that warm March night, they had everything ready to go. Once we started, I quickly found the coonhunting I was familiar with had changed a bit since the days of my youth. Gone were the old pick-ups with the dogs tied to the bed with leashes. Replacing those veritable antiques was a shiny new Ford truck with a stainless-steel dog box in the rear. The equipment was much fancier than I remembered. However, in

one respect, things hadn't advanced in the coon-hunting arena all that much. Instead of riding mules after the dogs were turned loose, we would walk everywhere we were going.

After a five-mile drive north of their house, Jonathon let the dog out of its luxury box and fitted it with a directional radio collar. The collar, which was on a specific radio frequency, helped Jonathon track the dog once it dissolved into the night woods. A small hand-held receiver with a directional radio antenna was scanned across the horizon in order to ascertain the direction from which the signal originated.

Once released, the treeing Walker sniffed around close to the truck, hiked his leg a time or two in typical canine fashion, and eased off into the bare-limbed red oak forest. A few yards out, unseen, you could hear his big paws crunching the dried leaves as he crisscrossed back and forth in front of us. Paul Wayne, Jonathon, and I leaned against a trio of big oaks and waited for the dog to tell us he had found a coon. The sky that night was inky black, filled with millions of dots of starlight. Listening for the dog to bark, we couldn't talk. All I could do while waiting was stare up and look for falling stars.

"Get after 'em, Crossfire!" Paul Wayne cried. With a bit of reassurance, Crossfire returned a bawl as if to say he would do his best.

Crossfire is an-all around sort of coondog. He is a competition hunter who travels all over the country to compete against other coondogs in field trials. He is also a stud whose breeding fees are a couple of hundred dollars per appointment. That may sound like a lot of money, but breeding rights for many dogs, male and female, can be more than that. In fact, I have seen ads for top-performing coon dogs selling for as much as $300,000.

After waiting for several minutes, Jonathon pulled out his telemetry receiver and scanned for the dog. He found a signal to the west of us. As we walked toward him, Crossfire started to bark. He was hot on a trail. A few more minutes later, he started barking with more enthusiasm. He had found and treed a raccoon.

Chugging through flooded fields and through the briars, we followed Crossfire's deep bawls. After what seemed like an eternity of walking through the woods, we found the dog. His paws were up on a tree and he was looking with excitement toward the big white ash's canopy. Shining the lights up, we spotted the coon nestled in the tree's fork about 20 feet up.

Crossfire barked, and barked, and barked. He continued barking until Jonathon walked up and put a leash on him. Pulling him away from the tree, we walked back to the truck. The coon, perhaps a little spooked, probably went and told his contemporaries about the adventurous night he'd had.

Paul Wayne and Jonathon are competition hunters so they often leave the coons alone once they are treed. That night's hunt was just practice for many upcoming competitive hunts the three will embark upon.

The foxhound is, perhaps, the quintessential hunting breed. Born out of England's misty hillsides, fox hunting began in America during colonial times, before the United States gained its independence. The first foxhounds were imported to Maryland in the June of 1650. Soon after, their numbers proliferated throughout the colonies and society's upper echelons widely adopted the sport. George Washington owned foxhounds and frequently organized hunts around the nation's capitol. Stories are even told of in-session congressmen running outside the capitol to watch a fox hunt passing by.

Fox hunting grew into the 20th century, and in 1907, the Masters of Foxhounds Association was organized to "set and maintain high sporting standards among its membership, encourage fox hunting, approve and register territories on official maps of fox hunting countries and settle disputes in regard to the same, register eligible foxhounds in a foxhound stud book, and improve the breed of foxhounds." The MFA is the primary sanctioning body for registered hounds, organized hunt clubs, and field trials.

Fox hunting has grown to encompass organized hunts all over the country. In fact, there are 171 organized hunts in the United States. Instead of chasing exclusively foxes, many organized hunts also pursue coyotes. This is due to the canine's wide range encompassing virtually all of the United States. Primarily, English and American foxhounds are used in the hunts, but some crossbred dogs are used. To be considered a purebred, an English or American foxhound must be at least 15/16 pure, although crossbreeds look essentially the same.

Today, fox hunting is fraught with the same traditions practiced when the sport first made its way across the Atlantic Ocean and onto the colonial landscape. The names of the hunt participants are as colorful as the clothing the hunters wear—white riding pants, black, knee-high boots, white shirt, and, depending on what aspect of the hunt they are involved in, either a red or a black coat.

Like a football team, members of the hunt have different responsibilities to make the team run smoothly. Colonel Denney, a retired United States Marine who runs Cloudline Hounds near Celeste, Texas, puts his daughter Susan and her husband Craig in charge of coyote hunts running across the rolling prairies northeast of Dallas. As huntmasters, they wear red coats that set them apart from others in the party. Their responsibility is to lead the hunt pack in following the dogs down trails, across creeks, and over the occasional jumps that are carefully built by the hunt club's members in border fences separating pasture from pasture. Other hunters in red coats ride out both to the sides of, and behind, the pack of 10-dog couples. (In a fox hunt, the dogs are divided into pairs and referred to as couples.)

Whipper-ins ride parallel to the dog pack as the hunt ensues. Their job is twofold; they keep the dogs together and steer the hounds in the right direction when the trail grows cold. The whipper-ins force the hounds to be more efficient hunters, because running together makes it easier to pick up and follow an old scent until it becomes hot again. When the whipper-ins keep the dogs together, the group of black-coat-clad hunters stays together and the hunt goes much more smoothly.

The red coats ride and manage the hunt through great teamwork. From a distance the dogs and the hunters look like a single unit as they move in reaction to the scent.

From a Chevy Suburban, Colonel Denney and I watched a group through binoculars. The Colonel, in his seventies, has a candor that bespeaks his many years of military service. He explained to me the etiquette of fox hunting from a lifelong perspective. He talked about his dogs' lineage the way most talk about first and second cousins. As he talked, I tracked the hunt party through a pair of 50-year-old binoculars he had bought in Japan while he was stationed there half a century ago. He told me about his adventures hunting with hounds in Arkansas, Virginia, other parts of the United States and even England.

The Colonel even told, jokingly, of when he first moved to the town of Celeste. People would stare with curiosity at the English-style saddles, tack, and attire he and his family would wear around the area on hunts and casual rides. In Hunt County, which is dotted with beef cattle ranches, western saddles are generally the rule for equestrians. Therefore, he explained, the change in equine scenery was refreshing.

We rode and talked for about an hour and a half before we saw a grizzled gray coyote running across the broomsedge bluestem-grass prairie with dogs and riders about 150 yards behind. For an instant, the coyote was exposed, and then he slipped into the deep brush lining a muddy creek. The hunt was effectively over.

The Colonel insisted that was OK. The Cloudline Hunt Club participates in the sport not for the kill, but for the hunt's traditions—and those traditions indeed run deep.

# lushing paniels

The athletic and result-oriented spaniel is a wonderful hunting companion. Wing shooters use spaniels to flush quail, woodcock and pheasants. They are also used to start fur-bearing game such as raccoons.

Believed to have originated in Spain, the spaniel found its way into British culture. It is mentioned in text dating from 300 A.D. The first North American English springer spaniel can be traced back to 1913. Due to selective breeding, it is one of the most popular modern breeds.

These alert and resourceful dogs are intelligent, loyal, and seek to please their owners. If there is game to be found they don't let the terrain get in their way. The following photos demonstrate these wonderful springer and field spaniel traits.

# $\mathcal{S}$easons of the $\mathcal{D}$og

A dog's year is much different from a human's year. We have all heard that a dog ages at a rate seven times that compared to people. In other words, one of our years equals seven dog years. That fact is well understood.

It has been said time and again that hunting dog owners go afield not in pursuit of game, but for the sheer pleasure of seeing dogs work. Kyle Allen, a Texas attorney and avid bird hunter, confided that sentiment in a cold duck blind one morning as a yellow Labrador retriever swam what seemed like a quarter-mile in pursuit of a downed duck. "Watch that dog work," said Kyle wide eyed. "That's amazing how he can find that bird. Man…watching these dogs work…now you know why dog people like to hunt so much."

A dog's year does not follow the same Julian calendar most of the world has followed for over 2,000 years. Instead, it follows a year governed by things like the first day of quail season, or dawn on a first morning duck hunt, or the full cry of a coonhound on a frosty December night.

# Fall

September 1st is opening day of dove season and the hunting dogs' equivalent to our New Year's Day. For some retrieving dogs, dove season brings a chance to reawaken a primordial urge to run and pick something up. Mourning doves are keen of eyesight and fleet of wing. Yet for some reason, uncamouflaged black and yellow labs seem invisible to them as they whiz overhead. Maybe the doves do see them, but they may not perceive a dog's silhouette as a threat—unless we can peer through the eyes of a dove, we will never know.

Late fall brings about the opening day of quail season. In the hierarchy of all hunters, chasing bobwhite quail is perhaps more steeped in pageantry than any other type of hunting, whether dogs are used or not. Quail hunting is a stately sport that brings out the best in antique guns, attire, and dogs. A covey rising over a statuesque pointer is classic hunting symbolism at its best. Dogs, inarguably, make the picture complete.

Also in the fall, retrievers take to the field in pursuit of waterfowl. Waterfowling is the quintessential sport in which retrieving dogs partake. With waterproof coats, webbed feet, and a propensity for swimming, Labs, goldens, and other retrievers are well suited for doing the hard work that comes with duck hunting. Although a high-spirited breed, it is amazing how a well-trained retriever can sit motionless in a blind and watch for ducks flying overhead.

In the duck blind, shotgun blasts rain steel shot bringing ducks spiraling to earth. With the command, the dogs spring forward and zigzag through a flooded timber or swim in a deep lake to pick up the delicate bird. Returning it to its owner, the age-old cycle that motivates man to train and take dogs afield is complete once again.

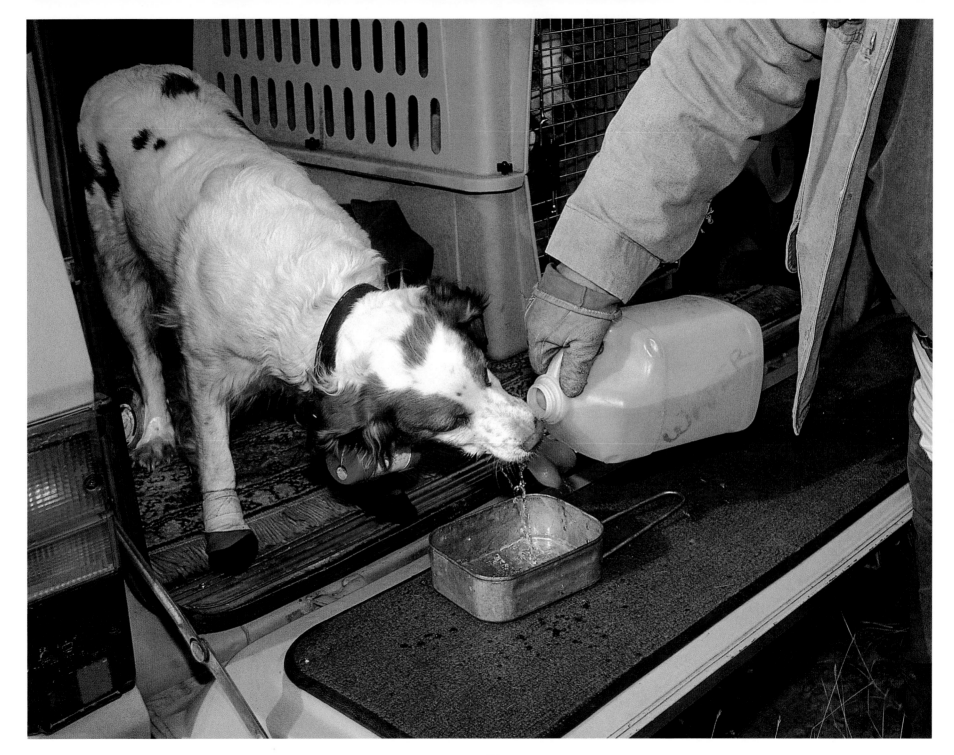

# Winter

For bird hunters, much of the season has waned come winter. The season past is remembered and great dog stories are related. If there is a season still open, new memories are created.

Winter is perhaps the best time to hunt other quarry. In many parts of the south, where coon-hunting tradition runs deep, winter is primetime for coon hunting. Milder temperatures bring about thicker pelts on raccoons. Where hunters harvest raccoons, pelts are of higher quality in the winter and bring a higher price when they are marketed to fur buyers.

Growing up, my entire coon hunting experience took place in the winter. The cold temperatures meant the dogs didn't wear out quickly. Fresh dogs meant we could hunt late into the night—often until 4 or 5 in the morning. Cold temperatures also meant that the dogs did not have to worry about ticks and fleas, and that we did not have to put up with buzzing mosquitoes or burrowing, itching, subcuteaneal chiggers.

Winter is a transitional time in the world of the hunting dogs. Some breeds wind down their year while others pick theirs up. If dogs could talk, I suspect they would tell you that hunting is always on their minds. They hunted for a living until humans domesticated the necessity out of them. It is in their blood and even deeper in their genes.

Yep, dogs think about hunting all the time. You can see it in their eyes.

# Spring

Spring is puppy time. Many owners breed their females so they whelp pups in spring. Spring pups have the opportunity to be nursed, weaned, and taken hunting in the course of less than a year. Before they are hunted for the first time, the business of being a pup always comes first. Puppy time is playtime.

Watching puppies at play is as close to Utopia as one can get. They wrestle and nip at one another. They growl, yap, and chew to their hearts' content.

Spring also signals a restful time for adult dogs after a hard hunting season. Days are spent lying around, soaking up sun, and thinking about absolutely nothing. Some spring dogs do not get to rest, though. Some owners continue the regimen of work by taking their best dogs to field trials—the ultimate in hunting dog competition. Dogs may retrieve, point, tree, and perform a host of other tasks related to the hunting ritual.

Spring dogs often become family dogs, too. Instead of strictly tending to business, spring dogs get to socialize more with family members and, in some ways, get to take on the role of a "normal" family dog—but not for long. Soon, summer rolls around and hunting season isn't far off. Thoughts turn to another season in the field, and another time to make memories.

Summer is a time of transition. Lazy spring days yield to warmer summer temperatures. Lethargic habits give way to an increase in activity for both dog and master. Summer means that hunting season is nigh and both have to be prepared. After all, pride and bragging rights will soon be on the line.

Fat put on by lazy dogs often gives way to a more lean and muscular shape as dogs are put through training exercises to build their cardiovascular and muscular endurance. A friend of mine uses a tennis ball and a rag to get his dog to fetch and retrieve, and also to get his dog's attention. The dog behaves as if it is play, but deep down you get the sense she knows what the play is all about. It won't be long before she gets to go afield once again.

Regimented training exercises may include practice pointing on pen-raised birds. Running through a field where wild birds may be found is another option for the preseason gun dog. Like hefty football players in summer camp, hunting dogs and their owners must take the summer months seriously if they expect to have productive hunts in the months ahead.

Summer is also a time when puppies, born in the spring and initially trained a few months later, get to take their first steps into the magical world of hunting. Many hunters and trainers put their best prospects through the minor leagues so to speak. They get trained like, and get to run with, the big dogs. Oh, they may point or retrieve, but at just a few months old, it seems to be more instinct that drives them to do it than training.

It does not matter, though. Puppies and grown dogs alike make hunting birds, coons, and whatever else, special. If it was not for them, who knows? Hunting may not be as popular as it is today. No one I know wants to find out.

5. *The better the dogs you hunt with, the better you will become.*
   Work with the best and you will become better. Always expect excellence from yourself and the people around you.

6. *Finish what you start.*
   A good dog leaves no quail in the brush just because it is tired. It keeps working and working until the job is finished. A dog that does not quit gets everyone's respect.

7. *Don't always take no for an answer.*
   Persistent dogs get their master's attention and get to go even when plans called for them to stay. Be persistent—you make your own luck by being where the action is.

8. *Bark, but don't always bite.*
   Stand up for what you believe in, but do it in a diplomatic manner. Bridges aren't always made to be burned.

9. *No matter how bad things get, never let your spirit become deterred.*
   Your spirit is one of your most precious commodities. Do not let the disappointment of a few mistakes paint a picture of what you will become. If puppies let mistakes stop them, we would never have good dogs in the field.

10. *Love being alive.*
    No explanation is needed.

# Epilogue

Many people who own hunting dogs will invariably tell you the same thing: the interaction with the dogs is more valuable than killing game. Although humans train hunting dogs, the dogs also train us. If we are willing to pay attention, they can reinforce life's lessons in a practical way. Here are 10 lessons we can learn from hunting dogs:

1. *Be happy with your situation even when things aren't going your way.*
   Watch a bird dog for a minute. They may bust a covey of quail prematurely or ducks may not be flying, yet the dogs are undeterred. They are thrilled to simply be alive and where they are at that place in time.

2. *Work hard, but play harder.*
   This is a no-brainer. Have you ever seen a dog with a used sock? They are in doggie heaven.

3. *Thank the ones who helped you get where you are.*
   Have you ever seen an ungrateful gun dog? Although it can't say the words, you know by a lick on the hand or a soft nuzzle that the dog loves you and is thankful you took them afield. We should take heed and thank the people who help us out along the way.

4. *Give respect if you expect to get it.*
   Good pointers will honor another dog that is on point first by not running up and flushing their birds—it is the dog's version of respect. If we watch them, we can learn a lesson from them.